Thoughts and Feelings

Thoughts *and* Feelings

Help

Written by Susan Riley
Photos by David M. Budd

The Child's World®, Inc.

Published by The Child's World®, Inc.

Design and Production:
The Creative Spark, San Juan Capistrano, CA

Photos: © 1998 David M. Budd Photography

Library of Congress Cataloging-in-Publication Data

Riley, Susan, 1946–
     Help / by Susan Riley.
         p. cm. -- (Thoughts and feelings)
     Includes bibliographical references.
     Summary: Simple rhyming text describes how it feels to give and to get help.
     ISBN 1-56766-670-1 (lib. reinforced : alk. paper)
     1. Helping behavior in children Juvenile literature.
     [1. Helpfulness.] I. Title. II. Series.
BF723.H45R55   1999
177' .7—dc21
                                                            99-28176
                                                                CIP

Up here in the tree!

Way up at the top!

Can you see it is me?

I climbed up too high and I can't get down. Please help me. Get me back on the ground!

Do you know
what "help" means?
I'll tell you now.
When I give help and
get help, this is how.

11

I help little kids
when they get into trouble.

I help with the snow,
and I use a big shovel.

I help set the table and
clean up my room.
I help with the groceries
and sweep with the broom.

18

And people help me.
They help me a lot.
They help when my shoelace
is tied in a knot.

People help me
read books...

and reach things up high.

And right now
they're helping me down
from the sky.

There's no doubt about it, helping makes me feel GREAT!

Now you try it, too.
There's no time to wait.

28

We should always help others. It's the right thing to do.
It's not very hard—
you'll see that it's true.

29

So do a good deed,
or help someone in need.
You'll find it's one way
to brighten your day!

For Further Information and Reading

Books

Berenstain, Stan. *The Berenstain Bears Help Around the House.* Inchworm Press, 1996.

Braybrooks, Ann. *Just Be Nice: And Help a Friend.* New York: Golden Books, 1998.

Davis, Jennie. *The Child's World® of Helping.* Chanhassen, MN: The Child's World, 1998.

Web Sites

For information about thoughts and feelings:
http://www.kidshealth.org/kid/feeling/

Fairy tales and stories about thoughts and feelings from all over the world: http://www.familyinternet.com/StoryGrowby/